MICHELLE OBAMA

By Joan Stoltman

Gareth Stevens
PUBLISHING

Please visit our website, www.garethstevens.com. For a free color catalog of all our high-quality books, call toll free 1-800-542-2595 or fax 1-877-542-2596.

Library of Congress Cataloging-in-Publication Data
Names: Stoltman, Joan, author.
Title: Michelle Obama / Joan Stoltman.
Description: New York : Gareth Stevens Publishing, 2018. | Series: Little
   biographies of big people | Includes index.
Identifiers: LCCN 2017020468| ISBN 9781538209295 (pbk. book) | ISBN
   9781538209301 (6 pack) | ISBN 9781538209318 (library bound book)
Subjects: LCSH: Obama, Michelle, 1964–Juvenile literature. | Presidents'
   spouses–United States–Biography–Juvenile literature. | Legislators'
   spouses–United States–Biography–Juvenile literature. | African American
   women lawyers–Illinois–Chicago–Biography–Juvenile literature. |
   African American women–Biography–Juvenile literature. | Chicago
   (Ill.)–Biography–Juvenile literature.
Classification: LCC E909.O24 S77 2018 | DDC 973.932092 [B] –dc23
LC record available at https://lccn.loc.gov/2017020468

Published in 2018 by
Gareth Stevens Publishing
111 East 14th Street, Suite 349
New York, NY 10003

Copyright © 2018 Gareth Stevens Publishing

Designer: Samantha DeMartin
Editor: Joan Stoltman

Photo credits: series art Yulia Glam/Shutterstock.com; Cover, p. 1 The White House/Getty Images News/Getty Images; p. 5 (main) Gage/Wikimedia Commons; p. 5 (inset) MCT/Tribune News Service/Getty Images; p. 7 Fotonoticias/WireImage/Getty Images; p. 9 Bloomberg/Bloomberg/Getty Images; p. 11 JIM WATSON/AFP/Getty Images; p. 11 Pete Souza/Wikimedia Commons; p. 13 JIM WATSON/AFP/Getty Images; p. 15 Chip Somodevilla/Getty Images News/Getty Images; p. 17 (main) Larry Marano/WireImage/Getty Images; p. 17 (bottom inset) Tasos Katopodis/Getty Images News/Getty Images; p. 17 (top inset) Feng Li/Getty Images News/Getty Images; p. 19 TIM SLOAN/AFP/Getty Images; p. 21 Drew Angerer/Getty Images News/Getty Images.

Printed in the United States of America

CPSIA compliance information: Batch #CW18GS: For further information contact Gareth Stevens, New York, New York at 1-800-542-2595.

CONTENTS

Boldface words appear in the glossary.

A Happy Childhood

Michelle Obama was the first African American First Lady! She was born in Chicago, Illinois, in 1964. Her father worked very hard even though he was sick. Michelle had to sleep in the living room with her brother, Craig, growing up. They didn't have a lot of money, but they were happy!

Michelle's brother Craig and mother Marian

So Smart!

Michelle's mother taught her to read by age 4! She even skipped second grade because she was so smart. Michelle went to a high school for gifted children, even though it was an hour away. She ended up with the second-highest grades in her class!

"I never cut class. I liked being smart. I liked being on time. I thought being smart is cooler than anything in the world."

- Michelle Obama

LET * GIRLS LEARN

Michelle went to Princeton University and then Harvard Law School, some of the best schools in the country! Her father died after she finished **college**, but Michelle kept working hard. Michelle became a **lawyer** and worked for the city of Chicago. She worked for a college and a **hospital**, too.

Making a Family

Michelle married fellow lawyer, Barack Obama. When her daughters, Malia and Sasha, were born, she worked less to care for her family. Michelle's mother, Marian, often took care of the girls. Later, Marian even moved into the White House to help raise Michelle and Barack's daughters!

At the White House

In 2009, Michelle became the 44th First Lady of United States after Barack became president. As First Lady, Michelle started **programs** to help US **veterans** and their families. She also worked to help young girls in school and high school students trying to go to college.

Everywhere Michelle worked in Chicago, she started **volunteer** programs. As First Lady, she wanted to **inspire** the country to volunteer and help others. Michelle had a big role in encouraging people across the country to volunteer through the United We Serve program.

the Obamas volunteering
at United We Serve

Michelle also worked hard to build programs in every state to help people get healthy. Her Let's Move! program was about exercising and trying new sports or activities. Her school lunch program made school lunches healthier so kids could do well in school.

Michelle even got food companies to agree to make healthier meals and snacks! At the White House, she planted a huge garden. She wrote a book to show everyone how easy it was to grow their own healthy food!

A Great Lady

After 8 years in the White House, the Obamas moved nearby so Sasha could finish high school with her friends. Michelle and Barack started the Obama Foundation in Chicago. She works hard for the programs they started in Washington, DC, every day!

21

GLOSSARY

college: a school after high school

hospital: a place where sick and injured people are given care or treatment

inspire: to cause someone to want to do something

lawyer: someone whose job is to help people with their questions and problems with the law

program: a plan of things that are done in order to achieve a result

veteran: someone who served in the military

volunteer: someone who does something without being paid to do it

FOR MORE INFORMATION

BOOKS

Gourley, Robbin. *First Garden: The White House Garden and How It Grew*. New York, NY: Clarion Books, 2011.

Pastan, Amy. *First Ladies*. New York, NY: DK Publishing, 2017.

Zumbusch, Amelie von. *First Family: The Obamas in the White House*. New York, NY: PowerKids Press, 2010.

WEBSITES

Michelle Obama on Twitter
twitter.com/michelleobama
Read what Michelle herself has to say on her public account.

Michelle Obama - The White House Vegetable Garden
biography.com/video/michelle-obama-the-white-house-vegetable-garden-33473690
Watch this short video about Michelle Obama.

The First Ladies
americanhistory.si.edu/firstladies-interactive/
Click images of former first ladies' dresses to read the stories of their lives.

INDEX